Advanced guide for cryptocurrency mining

Content

Why choose cryptocurrency mining? 5
How are cryptocurrencies mined? 11
What you should consider about cryptocurrency mining 13
Data to measure the profitability of cryptocurrency mining 16
The role of profitability calculators 21
The basic tricks for mining cryptocurrencies 25
Requirements for mining cryptocurrencies 29
Does holding cryptocurrencies create interest? 36
How to select the cryptocurrency to mine 40
All about a mining pool 42
Is it profitable to mine alone or with others? 43
What do web miners represent 48
Everything that cloud mining generates 52
The most popular ways to mine cryptocurrencies 55
How to earn income by mining cryptocurrencies. 58
How much can you generate by mining cryptocurrencies? 61
How to mine Ethereum 62
What you need to mine Zcash 75
Tricks for mining Monero through your computer 81
Is Bitcoin mining difficult? 90

The audacity to try or carry out more ways to generate income through cryptocurrencies is a frequent attitude nowadays because it is a more effective financial product than the traditional ones, thanks to the yield they provide in the long and medium term, that is why it is a productive choice in all senses.

An important leap in the world of cryptocurrencies is mining, although at the beginning it represents an activity and a concept difficult to understand or measure, so you should investigate this topic to quantify the potential of this path along with all the factors behind it at a financial level.

Why choose cryptocurrency mining?

A basic foundation that works to understand cryptocurrency mining is profitability, because it is an element that by measuring shows you the type of financial tool that this represents, so you can visualize it as a feasible method or not, and best of all is that you can analyze the viability of this option yourself.

However, in the world of cryptocurrencies you must assume that no way is 100% effective, nor does it represent a total degree of accuracy, although in this case you can use cryptocurrency calculators to estimate what mining represents, as long as you add criteria that are important to measure this item.

To continue investigating this medium, you must assume each of the qualities of virtual currencies, since the huge amount of cryptocurrencies is an invitation to explore everything behind each one to opt for the most beneficial way, this is a key point to know how to mine and recognize its profitability.

Luckily online you can find different calculators that work as a profitability meter, although at the end of the day this concept varies according to each case or according to each purpose, even when you start mining, every day that passes the profitability changes, and these points can help you to better understand this alternative:

1. **What cryptocurrencies represent**

At present, cryptocurrencies are mostly known as a virtual means of payment, thanks to the fact that it is a digital asset that cannot be touched, which is why it is clearly distinguished from the traditional financial system, without leaving aside the fact that transactions are carried out by means of encrypted transfers.

When going to a store or a restaurant it is possible to pay with peace of mind with any cryptocurrency you own, this means that it is a payment unit that is regulated autonomously, therefore it is different and does not follow any guidelines of any Central Bank or governmental entity on its control.

This type of decentralized financial product causes the price or value not to be modified by any bank, but the movements are susceptible to Peer to Peer exchanges, so it is a value that is not imposed by banks, since it follows the effect caused by the law of supply and demand.

It is a financial ecosystem where huge inflations do not occur, therefore the value that abounds in the market is not susceptible to manipulation, thanks to the fact that the users are the ones who generate these assets, in this conceptual point is where the figure of mining acts.

It should be understood that not only are users able to have full control over P2P, but their role is to generate money, since they are responsible for creating the cryptocurrencies by carrying out the mining process, and this type of creation generates a reward in return.

That is to say, miners can count on receiving some unit of this type of currency, as long as they are active in managing the mining so that the cryptocurrency stays afloat, it is like a kind of prize.

2. **Mining reliability**

Mining is a legal practice that has a high degree of security, but requires some considerations, such as the formation of a strong password so that the assets or cryptocurrencies can be safeguarded, without leaving aside that legality is materialized when both parties generate a transaction.

This means that the use of cryptocurrencies is up to each user, and it also depends on the type of cryptocurrency and the willingness of both to make the exchange, so that the asset begins to circulate by the management generated by the parties.

3. **Existing cryptocurrencies**

There are many cryptocurrencies today, so calculating and comparing the profitability of each is a complex job, plus each has its own distinction to produce income, for that reason they do not have the same profitability as it is a logical point, and causes it to be a must to learn thoroughly which one to buy and which one to have.

The consultation about cryptocurrencies is only generated when you carry out a previous research, either with the most popular ones such as Deeponion, Lifecoin, Dash, Dogecoin, Monero and others, the important thing is that you can inquire about each one with the help of some specialized portals.

Finding an asset that is profitable is a specific job or effort, but it can be filtered or determined according to the hardware you own, since mining equipment or tools are not easy to get and you need to go for an asset that is reliable, without leaving aside that ideal momentum capture to buy.

When you want to recognize which cryptocurrency to buy, you must know about the subject and find out as much data as possible about these assets, but without focusing on their profitability at a specific moment, but rather on the project behind them and what it implies.

4. **The action of mining cryptocurrencies**

Cryptocurrency mining is a way or a participation in the creation of coins, seeking a prize or payment such as earning a share of them, so it can be described as a type of reward, because miners can receive them without the need to buy this asset class.

Without the need to carry out any operation with cryptocurrencies, you can be the holder of them, for this reason mining is similar regardless of the type of cryptocurrency you choose, although depending on your project, the process varies completely.

How are cryptocurrencies mined?

To perform cryptocurrency mining it is necessary to fulfill some mathematical calculations, through the use of computing power, because you would be making your equipment available to P2P networks that are responsible for performing calculations, thereby processing transactions until the blocks are sealed.

Once any transaction of any cryptocurrency is made, there is a formation of a block, which must be sealed, for it to happen that way it is important to perform mathematical calculations using some computers that operate 24 hours a day, every day with constant connection and covering the time.

The aforementioned process cannot be covered only with a laptop, much less an old computer of basic use, but one of the fundamental requirements is to perform the mining process with high-end equipment that are powerful, since the performance demanded by the mining processes is high.

A powerful equipment for mining ranges in an average cost of 1,000 euros, since it is necessary to have or implement specialized devices such as ASICs; Application Specific Circuits, these are created or designed for mining for its high power or response to this task.

In this world you can find people who agree to create some cryptocurrency, as it is something possible to do through mining, either pool or cooperative, regardless of the modality, participants work in the same way to obtain rewards.

The greatest guarantee in mining is that if you have the power to work, you will be able to find and receive the rewards you are looking for, since it is the formula through which you can solve a block and obtain what you propose, it is not a requirement to be part of a pool or to establish a cooperative to mine.

The creation of cryptocurrencies is also possible without being part of a cooperative, although opting for an independent path means covering an additional or extra cost, for all that means the rent and the precise payment to reach the profitability margins.

What you should consider about cryptocurrency mining

To be part of cryptocurrency mining, you should not overlook the conviction that is needed, since starting can be a doubtful step for anyone, but without ignoring the requirements that are established within this medium, because you can invest for the best equipment and have decision, but still the profitability is very variable.

Each cryptocurrency varies the level of profitability, together with the effect of other factors that end up being determinant for this activity to produce results, in this sense the following points stand out:

- Equipment estimation and cost in combination.
- The competition that exists over the mining of that type of cryptocurrency.

- The price of electricity and the type of energy consumption when maintaining a 24-hour connection.
- The mining process must have the advantage of the cooling required by the equipment, in addition to the type of energy demanded.
- The profitability offered by the cryptocurrency at that specific moment.
- The type of cryptocurrency you wish to mine varies from one cryptocurrency to another.

This kind of factors open the doubt about the profitability of cryptocurrencies, but it is not an easy measure to define, it requires a deep study of the current moment, of the facts that may arise in the present, that is how the income you get through cryptocurrencies is manifested.

The energy expenditure also represents another measure to focus on how much you can earn, without forgetting the level of investment you make on the hardware to comply with the mining processes, on all these points a variable of profitability arises, but it always depends on what you are able to invest or what is profitable for you.

In order not to overlook any aspect it is essential to use specific calculators, as it works as a tool that processes each data, and it is kind of criteria that determine whether it is worth it or not, plus over time the costs of light or electricity also marks a clear path on profitability.

In addition, you must include the issue of cooling, and the need for additional equipment, to stand out from the competition, but to reach an optimal level of profit the main thing is to choose the type of cryptocurrency you want to mine, because it does not mean the same profitability for all.

Likewise, the profitability of a cryptocurrency is not the same from one day to another, the same happens when a week goes by, for this reason the support of calculators is a way to know if it is worth it or not, but you must have the necessary data to perform these calculations correctly.

If you want to closely follow the data that measure productivity, you should bet on a manual calculation, that way you can make the most of these tools, as a good use of the information you have at hand about the performance of this mining activity, but under reliable measures that generate an accurate result.

Data to measure the profitability of cryptocurrency mining

When you want to measure the precise profitability of cryptocurrency mining, you need to work with data that is reliable, as the calculators must obtain and work with filling in the boxes or corresponding criteria, as well as understanding that each cryptocurrency has its own profitability, but the bottom line is that it is for you.

In the midst of cryptocurrency mining, there may be users who either use a computer that is completely dependent on the payment of electricity, because they use someone else's supply that they do not have to pay for, and in this type of situation a greater economic benefit is obtained, it is a much clearer example that shows how every detail influences.

The determining elements for measuring the profitability of cryptocurrency mining are as follows:

1. **Hash rate**

This is one of the most important and determining elements of cryptocurrency mining, it is a type of hash rate that is used to represent the unit of measurement of the power with which cryptocurrencies are processed, this is one of the simplest definitions and you must master it completely.

This value works as an indication of the amount of computational operations that a mining equipment can carry out, if you do not know about this type of projection you can research about this topic online, to compare it or take into account the model of your equipment with the term "hash rate" or "mining", so you can get help.

2. **Electrical quantity or demand**

The type of electrical quantity refers to the consumption produced by the equipment you use for mining, considering that it is an activity that cannot be carried out by means of a low-end laptop or a gaming tablet, but it is about equipment that is really powerful and these produce a high energy consumption.

In addition to this, the type of overheating that occurs on the equipment, this generates that you must calculate the cost of electricity, and the consideration of including an air conditioner on the space so that there are no restrictions because of this issue.

3. **Cost of electricity**

This measure depends entirely on the type of fee you have to cover on the property where you are going to mine cryptocurrencies, the figure depends on what you consume as it is what produces changes on the price and at the same time on the productivity of this activity, because it is a continuous action and varies over the course of the months.

What you pay for electricity should be included in the profitability measure, where the rise or fall in consumption ends up being reflected on cryptocurrency operations.

4. Hardware cost

Beyond the fact that you invest only once in hardware, it is still counted on what is spent or invested, so what you spend at the moment must also be measured in the long term to determine the usefulness of each device, regardless of whether it is a one-time or constant payment, it is a variant similar to those of a gamer where upgrading is a must.

5. Pool rate

Cryptocurrency mining must be performed in different ways, this means that the pool mode is not the only one, but if you opt for this way it is necessary to include the pool fee, where a percentage to be covered arises, and this is demanded on the data of the calculator.

6. Software commission

The software commission is another factor to include in the calculator, although it is used as a point of comparison, it is not a mandatory aspect to have a result or a measure of profitability.

Once you can add these elements, any calculator will automatically give you a result, especially considering the type of cryptocurrency you chose and the value it has, but within these items you should not forget the difficulty presented by that type of mining, until it is equated with the reward.

This is the way to see the profitability of a digital currency, and above all the clarity to prefer other alternatives that are more convenient to raise your rewards, so you follow closely the steps that are more productive when investing, so it is an advantage to use the calculator to avoid missteps.

Another reason to estimate the calculator is that it allows you to establish a critical point about the type of cryptocurrency you are looking to mine, i.e. it facilitates this decision completely, given that you are practicing a close and real-time look at what it means to execute mining, in addition to the fluctuations that this entails.

Using the calculator on some websites helps you to choose exactly the best way, because you find out which one is the most profitable, as long as you fill in the criteria used to measure each alternative.

The role of profitability calculators

Each website varies on the design of the profitability calculator, but they usually provide the same functions, as long as you take into consideration not to overlook some factors, as the result will always depend on your understanding of what is involved in mining cryptocurrencies.

Some calculations do not recommend or include the value of the software, although this is a general aspect that is constantly repeated, and the calculation options are customized so that you get the most comfortable way, the essential thing is that you can make a calculation of the profitability in real time.

This way of comparison is useful especially to take the first steps in this field, looking for the mining that produces more bonuses, which at the same time can be the most difficult to mine, so there are many aspects that you should think about beforehand, under the analysis of these options:

- **CoinWarz**

It is known as one of the websites that generates easy access, because you only have to select the algorithm, so that you have the opportunity to fill in the sections that the calculator has, additionally it has updated suggestions about the best currencies, so you can have an idea about the profitable currencies of that moment.

Another point that is classified within this website, is the magnitude of income or profits that arise through the mining of that cryptocurrency, just click on any of the cryptocurrencies to display the price graph, or you can simply enter directly to the custom calculation of your data.

The most valuable thing is that these results generate or expose beneficial results, to take advantage of some opportunity, or decide based on the estimated rewards, using this type of tool is very simple, especially because it is not limited to being just a calculator, but offers queries on any cryptocurrency.

Normally popular cryptocurrencies such as Litecoin Mining Calculator, Ethereum, Dash, Zcash, Monero and others, are being applied on the website, you just have to fill in the criteria and depending on the cryptocurrency, the calculation of the type of earnings to which you can have access is generated.

- **CryptoCompare**

It is recognized as one of the best cryptocurrency profitability calculators, due to the wide availability of coins, through the main website you can visualize different coins along with the price, without leaving aside that it is an informative portal for the publication of news and tips.

This tool is interesting because the data is presented in a comfortable and informative way, so that any user can recognize it. To do so, you only have to enter the "markets" section, which is located at the top of the menu, where you can enter "Mining Calculator".

Once you have access to the calculator, you will be able to enter data such as hashing power, the energy consumed, the cost and also the pool percentage, all of this is automatically compiled to present the result up to changing cryptocurrencies with a single click at the top.

- **Whattomine**

Recognized as another of the most interesting websites to perform a profitability calculation, it is developed by WhatToMine to provide complete options, since a glance on this website provides a great amount of information about the most demanded cryptocurrencies.

Before any point of comparison, you can sort or filter the cryptocurrencies, until you decide and use the calculator, for this you can enter the web and touch the currency on which the estimate will be made, this enables a section for you to take into account useful information such as values, data and other variables.

In the same way the calculator will count with measures such as hash rate, energy, cost, and much more, these measures are the ones that automatically show the degree of difficulty to perform mining, because the value and every detail of this activity counts to prove that it is a promising option at a financial level.

The consultation on the most recommended cryptocurrency is a help for you, since you can invest following those results or try another one that is more productive, the intention is that the effort will produce profits.

- **CoinCalculators**

This is a platform that follows the same operation of the previous ones, and also incorporates the same functions, where its interface stands out because it is clean and effective so that any user can use it, it is not necessary to be an expert, for this alternative you will be able to visualize the information of any cryptocurrency.

The basic tricks for mining cryptocurrencies

Cryptocurrency mining is a joint participation, which facilitates the verification of transactions that take place on the network, this works as a stimulus on the issuance of cryptocurrencies, all this is familiar with the development of algorithms, where two algorithms stand out for mining to occur:

1. **Mining algorithm**

It is known as hashing algorithm, and it is expressly dedicated to the processing of data, for it requires a mining hardware that is based on the mining that employs the cryptocurrency you chose, especially when using ASIC devices that are developed to work with a single type of algorithm in particular.

2. **Consensus algorithm**

It is related to the agreement that exists on all members, i.e. the nodes that arise in a cryptocurrency network to contribute to its operation, for it arises the questioning of transactions that meet certain criteria of validity, in addition to the order of blocks in the chain and others.

In the midst of these algorithms, some features emerge, where the issue of consensus stands out, as it should be a popular measure over cryptocurrency networks, just as it happens with proof of work (PoW) and proof of stake (PoS).

- **What is required with the proof of work**

It is an option in which you have to work very little, because you do not work yourself, but the type of hardware you decide to use to mine the cryptocurrency you have selected, because Pow is known as proof of work, which means that it is a consensus that seeks solutions to impose on a riddle through mathematical calculations.

A miner seeks to get in a fast way the answer to the riddle that is presented, thus it is possible to add a new block of transactions on the chain, it is interesting because these answers are not provided by two miners, it is a situation that does not occur regularly.

The riddle that is dedicated on each block requires a specific solution to solve it, this occurs randomly, for that reason it is not something that can be easily predicted, it is a mechanism that prevents the double spending of any currency.

That is, double spending refers to the fact that once the transfer of the cryptocurrency has occurred, you cannot transfer it back to another person as if it had not been spent, solving the riddle of a block involves getting the reward it provides, but the challenge is in getting to the answer before another miner does.

The hardware needs to process high amounts of data, especially at high speed, so it is essential for miners to have powerful equipment and above all that is suitable for mining the cryptocurrency you have chosen, for this reason the proof of work is known as a consensus algorithm widely used in mining.

Among the cryptocurrencies that use this method, Bitcoin stands out, so you must master this algorithm to be able to mine it, besides incorporating some special software, likewise there are other digital currencies such as monero, zcash, ethereum and others, in the case of the Ethereum network this consensus is fully developed, but it is merged with the proof of participation, so it is a hybrid offering.

Requirements for mining cryptocurrencies

Cryptocurrency mining the first thing it requires is a willingness to learn, because it is a long road, as well as incorporating patience as a fundamental resource, the next thing is to focus on the type of hardware and software required, along with electricity and internet.

Similarly, each of these devices requires a cooling system, so that each hardware has a protection for its regular operation, in addition to the type of space where this activity will be carried out, the most important thing is to consider the electricity and internet services because they must be stable.

Mining needs to be consistent, when any requirement fails and the activity is interrupted, you will not be able to get the profits you expect, so you should think about covering the following points:

- **Hardware**

The hardware consideration is based directly on the equipment you need to mine the cryptocurrency you want, regardless of whether it is generic hardware, you can incorporate processors and graphics cards that allow you to dedicate yourself in a special way to mining.

The decision of the type of hardware depends on the mining algorithm used by the cryptocurrency you select, because the mining algorithm is the one destined to set the rules through which the encryption is produced and undoes the encryption as well, in order to have access or safeguard the information.

This means that the algorithm makes the message easy to decipher, until it becomes undecipherable data, this happens or is developed to ensure that it is impossible to repeat the same result with another type of message, so it is a network that provides security so that no digital currency is counterfeited.

In the midst of the type of hardware that a miner can use, and the amount of algorithms that can be used to mine, you can follow some examples as a reference to make the right decision about your equipment, in the case of Bitcoin, you should buy ASIC devices that is specialized to mine SHA-256 algorithm.

Similarly when you are looking to engage in Ether mining, what you should get is a dedicated GPU graphics card, without neglecting the use of a computer that has a power supply that is certified, and in the case of Monero, a good CPU processor is enough to carry out the mining.

- **The Software**

There are different types of software or better known as computer programs that help to mine cryptocurrencies, besides being an essential part, because for example in the case of choosing Monero, it is a program that facilitates the hardware to have contact with the network to which the cryptocurrency belongs in order to mine it.

Currently there are different types of software that change depending on the type of hardware used, and also on the type of cryptocurrency to be mined, one of the most distinguished are CGMiner and Claymore, the first option is the most popular because it is used by Bitcoin miners.

In contrast, the second option such as Claymore is used for mining ether, zcash, and other popular, additionally you must have a program to monitor the behavior and actions of the hardware so that you incorporate the settings or configurations that go hand in hand with your preferences.

ASIC devices such as Bitmain's AntMiner usually have their own software to perform some configuration and control the performance of the device, while some of them mine through GPUs by downloading additional programs such as MSI Afterburner or GPU-Z.

The performance monitoring of the mining rig is carried out through the website that belongs to the mining pool where you are mining, or you can implement the TeamViewer program, so that you can access the rig remotely from an external device.

- **Wallet or purse**

It is a key complement because it is used to receive payments when mining, usually you choose some hardware or cold as is the case of Trezor, KeepKey and others, as well as some application such as Coinomi, Jaxx, Wasabi and others, but online is also possible thanks to MyCrypto, Blockchain, among others.

The function of cold wallets is available through a store that sells this financial instrument, they are reliable electronic equipment, while those that are software are downloaded through the application stores that you have on your mobile device either through the App Store or Google Play Store.

Another option is to prefer the official website of the wallet, that way you get versions for all types of devices, in the case of online wallets, they are not as productive according to the vision of experts, because they are vulnerable to attacks by hackers, this happens the same way when it comes to exchange houses.

Some additional services can be used as a custody for cryptocurrency funds, this helps you to live with the risks that exist on the platforms by an attack, the intention is that access to cryptocurrencies is not compromised.

When you do not have private keys to the wallet, then you have no protection over those funds, causing them to be assets that are exposed to any incident, therefore it is a danger you should not run.

- **Refrigeration and air conditioning**

Everything concerning the conditioning of the place cannot be overlooked, because mining equipment requires special care about temperature, due to the fact that it is an activity that develops a high level of processing, causing the mining hardware to increase its temperature.

The risk of these devices overheating is high, since that temperature level can be so high that it contributes to the deterioration of the device, even causing it to no longer work. To avoid reaching that point, the first thing you should do is to investigate the type of temperature limit that the hardware supports.

Additionally you should evaluate the temperature to which the equipment reaches during the mining process, that way it will be easier to find a mining break-even point, this is known as sweet spot, it is an opportunity to mine as you keep your equipment immune to any overheating.

Preventing the hardware from overheating requires considering some aspects, first of all, you should think about the cooling of the area where the equipment will be, to incorporate air conditioners such as fans or heat extractors, the important thing is that they are compatible with the facilities that you are going to use.

On the other hand, the best way to cool your equipment is by means of liquid cooling systems, as it is an effective method to provide proper maintenance, this in combination with cooling is a timely response to work mining, but it also depends on the configuration that is implemented.

That is to say, the configuration used for mining has a lot to do with the power that is assigned to the heat extractors that are part of the hardware, in addition to the processing power is another factor to be estimated, sometimes for the welfare of the mining device, it may be advisable to reduce the mining power.

The intention during mining is to keep the equipment working for a longer period of time without interruptions, for this purpose, its capacities must be at their maximum, without presenting some premature failures that could threaten your income.

Does holding cryptocurrencies create interest?

Earning interest from a cryptocurrency fund is possible when it works as a protocol, since the cryptocurrency mining reward system allocates rewards to participants for accumulating and holding assets of a chosen network.

The purpose of this process is to help validate transactions, and is called Proof of Stake or PoS; Proof of Stake, this protocol does not demand high energy consumption in terms of transaction validation, and the generation of new cryptocurrencies.

The importance of performing the Participation Test is that you obtain an amount of cryptocurrencies to be accumulated, and for this reason it is an activity classified as mining, if you want to be a validator in this type of network with PoS, you must have cryptocurrencies that you can dispose of for this activity.

After you have the cryptocurrencies you must block them in the blockchain, in this way you can certify that you will not use these funds for any purpose other than the validation of transactions, also this is like a policy so that you have commitment and security to maintain a good performance in the network.

If you exercise any irresponsible or damaging action, you can lose all the digital coins, for that reason that pressure helps you to act well, in the case of the validator node selection will be added to the next block of chains that works in a semi-random way.

The more cryptocurrencies you designate for this purpose, the higher the chances of being chosen, i.e. you will generate more money. The popularity of this mining mode is behind the use of PoS on cryptocurrencies such as Peercoin, PIVX, Lisk and others, as well as being a more environmentally conscious practice.

Similarly, on certain networks that employ PoS, the PoW system is also implemented as a hybrid combination, as is the case with Decred or Dash, for example, this is a reference to be taken into account.

- **Requirements for mining cryptocurrencies using PoS**

The validation of transactions through PoS does not require high power consumption, especially when you are looking to mine BTC, ETH and ZEC, in the case of acquiring specialized hardware, you will not have to worry because it does not require this, by means of a regular computer and a hard drive that supports the copy of the blockchain, plus a stable internet you will be able to mine.

You do not need to manage an entire node to generate money with cryptocurrencies using PoS, there are also pools to work with this type of cryptocurrency, which work in a similar way to mining pools using proof of work, because they distribute profits according to the level of participation of each one.

However, there may be special requirements that are specific to each network, and when you choose a particular network there may be a need to take care of the maintenance of the validator nodes, although these are usually rules that are created to ensure the security and scalability of the securities, in addition to the expectations behind each cryptocurrency.

Through the earnings calculator of the StakingRewards.com portal, you can find some approximations about the prices of the cryptocurrency market, i.e. it allows you to know how much a validator node is worth according to the blocked units, and this causes you to know the type of earnings to be obtained on an annual basis.

When you participate with a validator node role in the Qtum network, you can find significant annual earnings, but these figures change depending on the value of the cryptocurrencies you are working with, especially in the midst of a volatile market.

How to select the cryptocurrency to mine

A key point that generates doubts about the profitability of mining cryptocurrencies is the offering of each one, i.e. the way to measure the interest and productivity behind it, and this can be measured thanks to some key variables such as the current price of the cryptocurrency in the market.

To this is added the cost of electricity over the area where you are going to mine cryptocurrencies, without leaving aside the mining power provided by the hardware you use, each of these data are important to have a record about the profitability of mining those cryptocurrencies.

That kind of vision or study can be followed through WhatToMine and CoinWarz, as a support on this selection process, so that you feel comfortable and confident with the return that mining produces in the long term, you can dedicate time and study to the evaluation, so that it is a project that you are committed to.

When dealing with new cryptocurrencies, the involvement of traders is crucial, in addition to the evaluation of security and function to exchange such cryptocurrencies effectively, you must also implement growth prospects of the project, in addition to the possible use cases and the functioning of the blockchain.

Access to hardware and software is also a vital means of mining, they are essential and therefore you can not fail to study them, each of these characteristics along with those of cryptocurrencies, help you make a clear decision, you just need to start from the generic to the more specific.

Start with a blank book or a document to write down everything you need to know about each cryptocurrency, think or study from a technical and ethical point of view, it is advisable to use a roadmap to mark the objectives you are looking to achieve, along with the time span you expect to achieve it.

In the case of the repository the code of that project; GitHub or GitLab, along with a website and a set of social networks that are dedicated to expose details about mining, with all the minimal details that this entails, that way you are going to know any innovation that developers are working on.

But setbacks also add up, because that directly affects the value and holding of them, so the more details you can find out about the cryptocurrency project, you can visualize its value.

All about a mining pool

A mining pool is known as a node that connects a group of cryptocurrency miners, to organize this activity as a teamwork to produce more money, because it merges an important mining power, elevated the measure of hashrate possessed by the participants that inhabit the network, as a single projection.

Instead of carrying out mining separately, everything is concentrated on cryptocurrency networks that operate by means of proof-of-work, by employing this algorithm, the consensus that exercises different form, because the participants of this type of mining groups distribute the power of decision to another who manages the entire node.

This is the way to have access to those possibilities of integrating more blocks to the chain until the expected rewards are achieved, in both situations as PoW or PoS, the pool receives the rewards or percentages that belong to the miner, i.e. a part is framed as a loot to distribute in a balanced and equitable way.

Is it profitable to mine alone or with others?

Normally before mining cryptocurrencies, you can question whether it is better to mine in a group or to do it on your own, especially to determine what is more convenient to have rewards that are useful for you, you should also take this type of decision seriously as it is a variation on the type of profit that mining produces.

What you should consider is that, if you want to mine cryptocurrencies of the size of Bitcoin on your own, you need to have the necessary hardware with the right power, as well as waiting for the generation of rewards on one side of the blockchain, which takes longer when doing it alone.

The productivity of working together arises because the power of a mining device is insufficient when compared to the hashrate of a complete network, for this reason you may not mine an entire satoshi on your own, in addition there are and are formed daily several cryptocurrency mining farms where they work as a team of thousands.

In view of this comparison or visualization increases the importance of the possibility of forming a mining group, to compete against the variants of this type of environments, to measure this premise you can follow a clear example with what are the networks of cryptocurrencies such as Bitcoin and Ethereum, as they apply the proof of work (PoW).

That consensus algorithm used, is the first mining node to solve a mathematical riddle, this is imposed by the network to integrate a new block of transactions, so that they pass to the blockchain, which produces a certain reward of cryptocurrencies, in the midst of this management can only hit a single result set for that riddle.

The proposal on the cryptocurrency network is to discover and use the only way to get that answer, so the power is key to count on the probability that a mining node can find solutions to the established riddle, but everything is based on the power of mining, to make a difference with the other mining nodes in the network.

A miner who has 5% of the global mining power that is developed in a network has the ability to solve a greater number of puzzles over another miner who has just 1% of the total hashrate, whereas when more miners join together, they can add up to 100% of the network's mining power.

As you have more probabilities in your favor, no doubt mining becomes more profitable, because each member of the group gets much more than he can get if he would do it on his own, this is an important insight for choosing to mine in pool and so it gains more popularity.

On the other hand, if you find yourself mining a cryptocurrency such as Monero, since it is classified as an anti-ASIC, i.e. it is suited to CPU and GPU mining, it would still be insufficient to mine on your own, as you may have little mining power when compared to the entire network, so opting for a pool is most appropriate.

Under the estimated measures of CoinWarz.com, whoever owns a gamer GPU with AMD- Rx 570 qualities, can invest more than 2,000 days to have the first mined block when doing it alone, that is to say more than 5 years during this process that can be higher or lower according to the values demonstrated by the network.

Moreover, when you have mined a block, you will get the full reward of the mined cryptocurrencies, but you cannot lose sight of the time it takes to reach that point, that is why it is highlighted that, through pool mining, you can receive a higher level of royalties for the productive power.

In some negative cases, the value of cryptocurrencies can be dramatically devalued by the time it takes to mine a block, which can result in you not being paid anything for participating in the network.

- **The form of payment in the pools**

One of the doubts about the pools is the distribution of mined cryptocurrencies, for which there are several payment methods, usually PPS (Pay Per Share), PPLNS (Pay Per Last N Shares) and FPPS (Full Day Per Share), DGM (Double Geometric Method), as well as other additional options.

Each payment option focuses on distributing profits equally, according to the mining power provided by each participant, although it is vital to note that the reward you can receive for mining nodes is made up of two parts, the first being the new cryptocurrencies that are issued when a new block is added to the chain.

On the other hand, there are the commissions that arise per transaction that correspond to the same block, but depending on the type of pool administrators, they can impose as a condition to keep the proceeds of the commissions and is responsible for distributing the new cryptocurrencies generated for the workers.

Pool administrators charge members a percentage of what they have mined, this is usually another way to maintain a fee for participation within the group, thus maintenance can be implemented for the pool, this is why mining in a pool is still a viable alternative.

To start in the world of mining, this is an option that is gaining strength, since you do not need to invest so much for the equipment, because mining on your own requires more power to be a profitable way, everything is relative or proportional to the total hashrate of the network, which demands a considerable investment margin.

What do web miners represent

This is a type of software that is installed over the code base of a website, this causes the visitor's computers to be able to mine cryptocurrencies, carrying out the installation of this kind of software can be done by the website administrator or some attacker who can hack the website.

Sometimes web miners are classified as a malware, because the software does not issue any kind of permission, but only executes, but it is not the purpose of the program, but it is part of the responsibility of whoever installs it, because it may include some warning so that authorization is requested before it is activated.

Web miners are employed as a type of power, but it requires a high level of responsibility, so that its functions are fair and can be taken advantage of by any online user, but this does not exempt that some inappropriate use can be generated on web miners.

A fraudulent way to use this alternative is to install it through the code base of a website, thus allowing mining to be carried out with the computer of everyone who frequents that site until the rewards for the mined are obtained, but it is illegal to carry out this process without authorization and it fits as a scam.

Likewise when such a program runs without warning, it generates a higher power demand on the computers of users who access the website, because cryptocurrency mining demands high CPU performance, especially on computers that are not designed to support this.

For this reason some computers may start to work slower, and in some smartphones this causes serious damage on their performance, as the thermal expansion used by mining may exceed the usual characteristics of the device.

However, this malicious havoc does not represent the full functionality of this software, because web miners are used for some right or positive goals, as some initiatives are registered that, if they request permission to mine through your computer when you are visiting the website, for some charitable cause.

Likewise over some websites you have the opportunity to choose the amount of processing power you wish to donate so as not to overload the CPU during mining, at the same time web mining is employed as a resource for paid subscriptions along with website advertising.

In the latter case, it is the same with charitable initiatives, because the user has the advantage of issuing or not the authorization so that the processing power may or may not be used for mining, but it corresponds to a business model that is in full development.

- **The type of cryptocurrencies you can mine with a web miner**

Normally about web miners, the Monero cryptocurrency is used, because it is an asset that can be mined by CPU as a much more profitable way, especially when you get a positive amount of computers that add to this purpose.

In addition, another reason to choose this cryptocurrency is its project, since it corresponds with an asset that is dedicated to ensure the privacy of transactions, this is important for most users, since with this software they will not be tracked nor will they spend a vulnerable moment with their security.

Everything that cloud mining generates

It is a service where you can rent the mining power, so you can receive the rewards you have generated, it can be understood under the action of carrying out mining, but from the hand of a third party, but this time it is a platform that offers a portion of the mined power.

But this way hides a variety of questions such as profitability, and if it is not better to use your own means to mine using your own hardware, to answer this kind of questions you need to take into account the same factors that have to do with the profitability of traditional cryptocurrency mining.

This means that the profitability of mining on your own and through the cloud is similar, but there is a detail to consider such as the risk of being scammed for investing in cloud mining, which does not happen when you do it on your own, but the advantage over cloud mining is that you do not have to invest in all the necessary equipment.

Instead of buying a mining equipment, this way you don't have to worry about electricity, cooling system and other similar variables, so you don't have to worry about maintenance and hardware care.

But a disadvantage to consider is that this is a scheme where the risk of fraud is high, because the mining power used and provided by the platforms originates from farms that are part of the companies and therefore it is complicated to verify that they comply with all the mining power they generate.

In addition to this, some contracts have clauses about the cancellation of the service, in case the cryptoasset prices in the market are not beneficial for them, this is a risky breach for anyone, and it is impossible to ignore, this generates interest to discuss the fear of scam.

Normally what is most debated in this type of investment is security and reliability, to answer this it is vital that you analyze the background of the cloud mining platform in which you are going to invest, because it is a business model that emerges as an innovation in the mining environment.

The truth is that there are some cases of latent scams, so the reputation of this business model can be tarnished, but one cannot omit the number of platforms that offer this type of service, where the level of trust they have thanks to their flawless operation is demonstrated.

In the middle of the ecosystem of this platform and its users you can decide for this type of companies, one of the first dedicated to this purpose is CEXio, but the most popular is Genesis Mining, in this world a business model similar to cloud mining, where the mining power is not rented from a company but from other miners.

These platforms work as intermediaries for users who want to acquire the processing power, and others who are looking to sell it, this shows how many people exist wanting to mine cryptocurrencies, but do not have the resources to meet that goal, because the acquisition of mining hardware is high.

On the other hand, other people have state-of-the-art mining equipment, but are not very attracted to mining, which is why platforms such as NiceHash and Mining Rig Rentails provide or create a hashrate marketplace, thus presenting a high compatibility between the needs of the two groups of people mentioned above.

The main advantage of these media is that they are platforms that do not have their own hashrate, and the best thing is that you can evaluate in advance the reputation and comments of the mining community.

The most popular ways to mine cryptocurrencies

When mining cryptocurrencies it is necessary to recognize certain basic aspects, as has been mentioned repeatedly, the key point of all this dynamic is the blockchain technology, since it is what facilitates understanding the composition of this market, which in the first instance can be complicated to understand or master.

The reality of this process is that it requires information mastery, because learning to mine is a progressive phase, where the user contributes to the decentralization of this type of assets, since mining is based on the verification of the transactions that are carried out with the coins so that they enter the digital ledger named blockchain.

This ledger is managed on the blockchain as a database, which has the quality of being encrypted and is modified thanks to a cryptographic hash, i.e. the calculation that is implemented to encrypt each block, and it is also an incorruptible medium, since the database cannot be changed.

It cannot be forgotten that the cryptocurrency environment is decentralized, where the people who are dedicated to registering this type of operations on the blockchain network are the ones who acquire the denomination of miners, since they are the ones who write down within the blockchain database.

To fulfill the main function of the miners, a computational power is implemented to solve some algorithms that encrypt the blocks and transcribe the transactions on these blocks, this computational power helps to determine the cryptographic hash, this is a calculation that seeks to encrypt the operations so that they are not manipulated.

As such computational power is rendered, each miner will be rewarded with cryptocurrencies that come from the blockchain network that they are in charge of keeping under operation, this is developed by means of the following modalities:

1. **Cryptocurrency mining with video-GPU cards**

It is recognized as the first type of mining that is performed, and its development is due to the need to mine Bitcoins, miners using GPUs are dedicated to using the computational power that video graphics cards have, so they can solve computational problems that arise in the network.

But when computational power is not available, which causes blockchain networks that have GPU mining, higher power levels are required or demanded for successful mining to take place.

2. **Cryptocurrency mining with ASIC machines**

An ASIC machine, refers to an Application Specific Integrated Circuit", the creation of these has been especially for the mining of cryptocurrencies, for that reason they have a greater computing power compared to video cards, also as time passed that power has been growing.

This means that the increased level of difficulty of mining on blockchain networks is compatible with this type of equipment, to this day ASIC equipment continues to be used for mining cryptocurrencies, especially Bitcoin.

How to earn income by mining cryptocurrencies.

Doubts arise about the way in which money is earned in cryptocurrency mining, because not all participants can obtain rewards, so the first step is to work with some specific logarithms for each asset, in the case of Bitcoin the Proof of Work must be used.

What you need to know is that the blockchain network rewards the miners who create the blockchain that is valid and long, this has the name "Block Reward", or in English this means block reward, to cover the user's participation on the network to keep it running honestly.

A long and functional chain uses or requires a higher level of computational power, so the network seeks to generate Bitcoin and provide the corresponding rewards, to this effort is added the level of competition that may arise to generate the longest block, and for this it is necessary to have the performance of a mining farm or being part of a pool.

The computing power together, generates better results, it is also more economical because the investment is reduced, so when you plan to mine any cryptocurrency you must measure the level of investment to get to have that computational power, which is necessary to compete against other high consumption equipment that are part of the network.

To consider being a miner in a blockchain network, is to understand that this has a particular cost that you must cover to enter, this refers first of all to the computer equipment connected to the network, without leaving aside the amount of resources consumed by these devices, for the energy required for 24 hours a day every day.

On the other hand, the cooling system is a necessity because the equipment is on for a long time, which in turn adds to the power consumption of the cooling system, this is a clear motivation for the establishment of mining farms, especially to avoid the cost of electricity in places where it is free.

The special side of this activity is due to the mining equipment, this has a minimum cost of 395 dollars and a maximum of 1,316 dollars, although to this is added the value of the power supply, where you should not skimp on expenses as it is an important piece.

How much can you generate by mining cryptocurrencies?

In the calculations of cryptocurrency mining profits, it is vital to add or consider what it represents to invest for a mining equipment, as they are fundamental resources for this activity, but they modify the profitability of such activity in some cases, and to generate more money, you should think about investing at the beginning.

To measure the results or incidences of profitability, you should follow the advice given at the beginning such as the use of calculators, after that you can combine your performance and the frequency with which you will mine, but the amounts of cryptocurrencies are not exact.

Throughout the time that mining is managed, many variables may change, especially those related to the cryptocurrency itself, on the other hand, the estimate is presented in a gross value, but the cost of electricity consumption and the options to keep the equipment running for a longer time with proper cooling must still be reduced.

How to mine Ethereum

No matter if you do not possess enough knowledge, you can discover detail by detail what Ethereum mining represents, for this you must keep in mind the key features behind this cryptocurrency and about the mining powers, in this case it is an asset that dates back to 2015.

Ethereum is defined as a fully decentralized software platform, and is more than just a platform, as it owns and implements programming language, i.e. Turing complete, which means it runs through a blockchain, to provide help to developers when using Smart Contracts and distributed applications (Dapp).

By means of this kind of platform it is sought that frauds are put aside, without downtime or control by third parties, Ether is known as the cryptocurrency that uses the Ethereum platform, it is known as a token that allows to pay transaction fees and some calculation costs.

The power of Ether has grown to the point of being one of the second most important digital currencies after Bitcoin, which is why developers use smart contracts to receive, store and send Ether to other developers as well.

This means that ether is a motivation for developers to create and deliver better applications for the Ethereum platform, when it comes to payment means this is the way.

- **Start mining Ethereum**

Mining by Ethereum is simple, so it gains a higher level of relevance, but the basic thing is to know how this type of mining works, but it follows the same dynamics of Bitcoin mining where mathematical equations are solved by means of hardware ideal for this purpose.

The participation of miners from all over the world on Ethereum is a notorious fact, and useful for the network because they are people who invest their time in solving complex mathematical puzzles, when they get the answers about such cryptographic problem the miners can integrate the blocks to Ethereum blockchains.

That is the core dynamic to get the rewards you are looking for, once the miner solves an equation, he can count on getting 2 ETH for each block, to this must be included some transaction fee added to that block, but it is only possible to create the amount of 18 million new ETH per year.

There is no limit on the total number of tokens issued, but Bitcoin has a finite number of tokens, which is why there are different ways to mine ETH, such as the following:

1. Solo mining, which is based on solo mining.
2. Being part of an ETH mining pool.
3. Cloud mining.
4. Create your own mining pool.

In the case of the latter option, which has been described as one of those with a high level of competition, it is a type of mining that requires investment in order to mine a really significant amount.

- **Mining Ethereum by means of specific hardware.**

In the case of Ethereum mining hardware or mining rig, it is a machine that complies with a special design to mine this kind of cryptocurrency, mining rigs are described as a set of equipment consisting of a power supply, motherboard, GPU or graphics card and a cooling device.

Generally speaking you can mine Ethereum by CPU and also with GPU, CPU mining rigs have a CPU processor to implement complicated algorithms to find solution to the blocks that are part of the blockchain, CPU mining rigs are the most popular for miners.

The passion for mining rigs is based on the fact that they are cheaper and easier to use, you only need to have a computer, but the downside is that it is a much slower way of working, so you can know and consider how to mine ethereum by means of special hardware or GPU.

A graphics processing unit helps miners generate a higher level of hashing power, in the case of GPU mining rigs apply graphics cards that do not run CPU-like algorithms, but at least manage to complete mining processes through closed networks.

GPU mining rigs operate at a higher level than CPU mining rigs, but the only thing you need to consider is that they are very expensive, that kind of performance quality can range in the thousands of Euros.

It is for this economic reasoning that they choose the cheaper alternative, however, this affects performance because mining requires specialized hardware for you to make a profit, even if that means facing some operating costs.

The best hardware models for Ethereum mining are as follows:

1. Radeon RX 5700 XT

The Radeon RX 5700 XT with a triple dissipation inclusion, this is one of the best cards for those who want to be ETH miners, because it allows to meet a measure of 660 Mega Hash, also uses up to 68w per card, which comes to 0.16 euros per day, representing a cost that is estimated at 400 and 500 euros.

2. **Nvidia GeForce GTX 1070**

The Nvidia Geforce GTX 1070 card is recognized as one of the most chosen graphics cards, especially by gamers, but it also works to develop mining, for this reason it is an alternative to consider for the mining of that cryptocurrency to be carried out.

The main quality is that it is able to provide a very high hashing rate, without requiring large amounts of electricity.

3. **Nvidia GeForce GTX 1660 Ti**

It corresponds to a favorite option because it mines up to 30.5 Mega Hash per card, demands a general measurement of 68w, and has a cost of less than 200 euros, this is a card that is worth the popularity of the brand as well as the power that equals an NVIDIA for a lower cost.

- **How to mine Ethereum from a pc**

If you want to mine from your own pc, without leaving home, this is a possibility that you can take advantage of by means of the following steps:

1. To mine Ethereum on Windows, you must have Windows 7 64-bit minimum, or some later version.
2. In the case of mining, a PC with 4 GB of GPU memory is required, in addition to a minimum of 4 GB of RAM system memory, plus the stability of the Internet connection, so as not to lose power when you are mining.
3. The current version of your GPU drivers must be installed.
4. Download the necessary software to perform the mining function, for this there are many Ethereum mining programs.
5. Modify the Windows settings, such as the virtual memory size to a measurement of 16,384 MB, then go to the Windows power settings, and then you can disable the sleep mode. Once this is

done, you can go to the Windows Update settings and turn it off, because if you use Windows Defender and an antivirus, it can interfere with the mining program by classifying it as a threat.
6. Select a mining pool that matches your preferences.
7. Change the .bat file of the mining program according to the instructions you have received in the selected mining pool.
8. Create and prepare a wallet to store the ethers you earn.

For each operating system there are specific steps that adapt the computer to the mining process, you just need to understand the special way to manage that type of system, as with a Mac.

- **Mining Ethereum with Mac**

The mining community has no empathy for using a Mac for mining, as it may not be a worthwhile choice, because the most effective mining software for Ethereum does not have a version available for this type of operating system, but you can use Graphical User Interface (GUI) such as Minergate.

In the case of using Minergate as a substitute, you can implement the following steps:

1. Download the software from the Minergate website.
2. Sign up for an account.
3. Log in to the software using the account you have created.
4. Start mining Ethereum.
5. Although mining is not available for use on Mac.

In view of the limitations of this operating system, it is not the way to go to be part of the mining world.

- **Software to mine Ethereum**

The list of software to mine Ethereum works as a help to clarify and take the most appropriate path, but above all the one that turns out to be better at the level of performance, you can consult the following:

1. **Claymore**

It is compatible with Windows and Linux operating systems, without leaving aside that it is one of the best for mining on Windows 10 above all, but it is still an effective program for mining, because it has double Ethereum miner that facilitates the extraction of cryptocurrencies with algorithms without decreasing the hash rate.

The main quality of Claymore is that it allows to carry out mining of other cryptocurrencies above Ethereum, the mining commission that is set is 1%, in case of selecting dual mining, the commission increases up to 2%, also the download process is simple.

2. **Ethminer**

It is a well-known software for Ethash GPU mining, which facilitates mining all those cryptocurrencies that are submitted under the Ethash algorithm (Ethereum, Ethereum Classic, Expanse, Musecoin and others), it also presents a wide compatibility with Mac, Windows and Linux.

It has a special design to work with Nvidia graphics cards, and stays on top of Ethereum's best mining software rankings for Windows 7 and Nvidia.

3. **MinerGate**

It is considered as one of the best software to perform Ethereum mining for those who own Mac, likewise offers miners the ability to extract BTC, Monero, Zcash, Litecoin, and other tokens above Ethereum, the functionalities have a commission that varies from 1% to 1.5% depending on the digital currency.

The handling of this software is simple, because it is useful for any novice to start in the world of mining, also has the options translated into different languages.

4. **CGMiner**

CGMiner is considered as an Ethereum mining software that fulfills basic and free actions, it is written in C++, therefore it fits with most platforms, by means of a simple interface to take command, this causes that it can work across different pools and mining devices.

The interface designed for users and the adaptation of the commands does not generate problems, it also has accessories such as the Ethereum mining calculator, which is an aid to manage and control the hash rate, that is to say, every data that interests you is at your fingertips.

The design that CGMiner has is based on Ethereum mining pool software, this is implemented on GPU as a kind of advantage for beginners to grow in this medium, they only need to enter the username, URL, password and choose the mining pool, with the computer hardware applied automatically.

5. **Geth**

It is a development by the Ethereum team, it is considered as one of the original miners, because it is the one that allows to transfer the funds over different directions, to show the block history and to generate the contracts, this is compatible or functional with Windows and Mac.

6. **Phoenix Miner**

It refers to an Ethereum mining program with a short trajectory, but at the same time innovative because its latest version presents compatibility with dual mining, which makes simultaneous mining between Ethereum and Ubiq a reality.

The ways to mine Ethereum mention the way of pools, which for many represents a huge amount of doubts that can be solved by means of the following details discussed:

- **Mining Ethereum with pools**

Based on the huge amount of miners that concentrate on ETH tokens, it becomes a more complex activity, especially to reach that reward that is provided by a mined block, this allows each miner to have a low chance to solve an equation and obtain the reward.

That is the main motivation for many people to select a mining pool, which is a group of miners who are dedicated to sharing efforts, in order to have equally distributed rewards arising from the cryptocurrency mining activity.

Through a mining pool you can find a server that shares a mathematical equation, in a smaller operation to be distributed among the computers that are participating, once the users that are connected solve a block together, the reward is distributed proportionally, based on the power contributed by each user.

Through poolwatch.io the best mining pools are published, where Sparkpool, Ethermine, F2Pool, SpiderPool, and Nanopool stand out, the important thing about this is that you can choose an Ethereum mining pool that possesses attractive pool hashrate level, pool reputation, and commission rate.

However, you cannot overlook that there are many ways to mine Ethereum, these are not the only ways, and you can find an alternative where it is faster to get the token.

What you need to mine Zcash

The general requirements for setting up a Zcash mining system, advises to consider the use of AMD graphics or NVIDIA graphics, as it is a recognized and recommended hardware for the type of system behind the cryptocurrency, this is useful to know because of the popularity of cryptocurrency mining.

But the first step to make any decision or preference is not to not know what it takes, so you can count on a mining rig, but this happens when you gather the necessary components, this can be seen in a minimal measure so you can concentrate on what it takes to mine Zcash and analyze the profitability.

1. **Base plate**

The motherboard is the critical point to perform cryptocurrency mining, so it must be selected thinking about the importance it has, for this you must take into account that before selecting the motherboard you must know the number of graphics cards you are going to install and based on that number the motherboard is chosen.

One of the most striking is Biostar TB250-BTC which is used for six graphics cards, has a value of around 90 euros, while the Biostar TB250-BTC PRO is designed for twelve graphics cards for a cost of 250 euros, so based on your capacity you can go analyzing one by one, or look for others on the market.

Currently this type of motherboard is designed for Intel processors only.

2. **Processor**

The processor corresponds with an affordable alternative, because you don't need a very sophisticated processor, using the simplest Intel Core i3 is enough, by means of the Core i3 6100 you can start mining and it is one of the most chosen because its average value is 100 euros with heatsink.

That processor size is enough, since the processor is not demanded so many loads, but all the performance of the mining load, has much to do with the graphics, although you should take into account that there is no motherboard for mining that is done in AMD processors, so they are not an option.

3. **RAM memory**

At this point the decision can vary, as long as you can start from the minimum size of 4GB of RAM memory, as it is a sufficient size for this kind of systems, you can also prefer one module or two modules, but it is best to go for the second option to have Dual Channel settings.

It is advisable to keep in mind the purchase of memories that have the heatsink included, because this improves the performance of the memories, and if you want to get rid of the system later, they are more in demand when selling them as a second-hand item, but it is advisable to invest in a DDR4 RAM.

4. **Storage**

The field or what refers to the hard disk drive, it is always better to opt for an SSD that has a cost of 60 to 65 euros, likewise you can think of SATA as M.2 SSD 120GB, this is enough so that at any time you decide to retire you can sell the device without problems.

Maximum performance can be obtained by selecting a 500 GB or 1TB mechanical hard disk, depending on what you are most interested in, and in any case you can split it and set up a Storjcoin server to recover your investment.

5. **Power supply**

This is one of the points that may represent a higher cost, but it is less than the investment to be made on a graphics card, at this point you can invest up to 200 euros for one that has 80Plus Gold certification, along with a minimum power of 1000w, in the case of having six graphics cards, you will need two power supplies.

What is sought is that they are capable of supporting three graphics cards each, the consideration of the Enermax Revolution 87 of 1000w is estimated at 180 euros, and is one of the most estimated to perform mining, additionally there is the Chieftec Nativas of 1250w which is priced at 230 euros, both support three graphics cards.

6. **Graphics card**

It is a key element to perform mining, if for example you are interested in Ethereum, you may prefer AMD graphics, especially the RX 570/580, but the profitability of this option is not yet proven, instead Zcash mining is much better with NVIDIA, plus it is a graphics compatible with other cryptocurrencies.

To define the type of graphics you should always think about the type of cryptocurrency you want to mine, in case you continue with the intention that it is Zcash, you can try the best NVIDIA graphics such as the GTX 1060 for its price or GTX 1070 for the mining power, but if you want to mine at the last level you should choose GTX 1080 Ti.

7. **Riser**

The riser is what you need also to form a mining rig, this along with other elements should be purchased, under the concentration that you buy version 6 of this type of accessory, while still evaluating the type of features it provides, protection is also a useful value.

The overall investment of all these aspects is around 3,000 euros, but has an estimated return on investment in six months, but it all depends on the value of cryptocurrencies, without leaving aside that one month can be more productive than another, and the care of the equipment to keep them cooled.

Tricks for mining Monero through your computer

The emergence of Monero mining is curious, because it is one of the mining that can still be done by a CPU or processors, so it is a simple alternative compared to the whole wide mining market that exists, so it is a good opportunity to start.

Mining this type of digital currency will help you become familiar with the environment of this activity, it is an adventure with a lot of motivation because Monero is one of the best 20 cryptocurrencies at present, thanks to its project that presents scalability qualities.

Starting in any type of mining demands commitment to learn and improve, so before you start you must consider that it is a time investment, and you need to comply with some special measures that are part of this kind of activity, one of those aspects is the technical mastery of this type of process.

On the other hand, you must have a source of electricity supply that is profitable, since the mining process requires a continuous energy demand, therefore the mining process requires investment to obtain the necessary power to obtain rewards.

Taking care of the computer equipment is a useful measure as well, and freeing yourself from the pressures, it is best to start mining with a much more open view to what happens without anticipating the results, but it is always possible to learn to take in your hands the possibility of generating rewards on mining.

First of all, when you choose this kind of mining, you must have installed the most recommended mining software such as GNU/Linux, since it has open source codes and that in turn decreases the problems of virus or any other vulnerability, but you can use Windows as an easy way to start.

- **The use of the RandomX algorithm**

The development of mining requires knowledge of the development of the RandomX algorithm, because it does not require any type of special machine such as ASICs, so it is an advantage so that more people can get involved, this is an algorithm that is responsible for integrating randomness to the processes that are managed in mining.

These types of functions make it difficult to manufacture ASIC devices that decrease the decentralization of the cryptocurrency ecosystem.

- **Requirements for mining Monero**

The first thing you should think about when you are looking to be part of this type of mining is the computer equipment because it is what will be used to perform the main activity of mining, this type of equipment can be a PC, laptop or a professional laptop, the important thing is that you can work 24 hours a day, 7 days a week.

Similarly, when you have the best technical characteristics, you will have a much better mining performance, the minimum you should implement is a CPU that has a 64-bit operating system either Windows or GNU/LINUX, which has 4 threads or CPU core, 4 GB of RAM, in combination with a good broadband connection.

The equipment must have a software specialized in Monero mining, the easiest and most frequently used is XMR-Rig, in the same way you must have a Monero wallet to receive the deposits that are part of the mining activity.

- **The steps to mine in Monero**

In order for you to be part of this process without any problems or confusion, you can follow this basic step-by-step until you complete this process:

1. **Create your wallet**

The first thing you should do is to create a Monero wallet, so that deposits are not a complication and can be safe, that way you have the peace of mind that the mining activity will not be in vain, for this you can use the wallet offered by the official website of Monero, just enter the Downloads section, and select GUI Wallet.

When you are on this section, you must pay attention to the requirements of having Windows 64 bits, because it only works with a 64 bits system, so if you do not comply with this, it means that your PC will not support the development of the software, but if you have it, you just have to follow the instructions on the website to form the wallet.

2. **Start the wallet**

Once you have downloaded the wallet, you only have to run it to select the language, and then click on continue, to select the execution mode in which the wallet will be, it can be the simple mode that uses the wallet as a custody and connects with other nodes, or the bootstrap mode that carries out the creation of a local node that stores the blockchain.

Finally, there is the advanced mode, this is intended to provide more functionalities, this is an expansion of the mining, which allows you to create on your own the wallet, and then provide you with the seed phrase data, that kind of data must be well stored accurately, if you lose them you are granting access towards your wallet.

Once you have written down that kind of data, you can click on create wallet key, where you must choose something that you will not forget, to proceed with the default installation when all the configuration is done, so that you will set up the wallet to keep it working.

The synchronization process is a measure that you can set up so that you have everything up to date, this step is completed automatically and you will not have to worry about anything.

3. **Download mining software**

Downloading the software is what opens the way to the mining activity, because the computer equipment will be put in place so that you have your own mining center or space, through XMR-Rig, thanks to the open code of this type of program you can find all the documentation for you to download.

The configuration of the program can be carried out without any problem, and allows you to have your earnings at the same time, what you must visualize is the type of version you need, it all depends on the operating system you use.

4. **Choose the mining pool**

Having covered all the above, it is time to select the pool where you want to mine, to carry out this step, you must consider that this server is close to your location to follow the same line of performance without problems, because a pool must maintain the mining activity in a stable way.

Package delivery failures are what no one looks for or expects in a pool, for that reason the best thing you can do is to be realistic to assume the pool that suits you best to make profit, you can log on to moneropools.com to read a list of mining pools.

5. **Adjusts the mining software**

This step is close to the mining adventure, you just have to enter the wizard configuration section to perform some key steps, firstly, you have to click on "New configuration", then on "Add pool", that way you can choose support if you placed a wrong pool and then on the custom option.

When you place the custom option because you do not get the pool, a drop-down menu appears for you to enter the complete data that you can request from the pool to enter the pool, in case you need more support you must choose supportXRM to complete the wallet information and the name of the worker as a type of identification.

Therefore, you can carry out the backend option to indicate the way in which you want to mine, being Monero in that part you must place "CPU", then at the end you can count on the final configuration that allows you to use the selected pool with the options set so that the money generated goes directly to the wallet.

- **In case of configuring the miner**

An easy way to configure XMRig for uninterrupted operation is by means of the config.json file that is designed for this purpose. To do so, you only need to open the file using a text editor or notepad, then delete the content and copy the one provided by XMR Wizard.

Once you have completed these steps, all you have to do is double-click on the xmrig executable option to start mining without any problem.

6. **Optimizes mining equipment**

It is a step that advanced users understand better, but you can dedicate yourself to learn how to optimize your CPU as that allows you to do better in terms of performance, the essential thing is that the mining application follows command lines, which can be modified to follow certain commands that are not preconfigured.

This kind of alternative varies a lot depending on the power of your computer, so you will start to notice the results of the mining activity in a short time, since you will be increasing the performance.

For this reason Monero mining is presented as one of the simplest, compared to other cryptocurrencies the adaptation of equipment are minimal steps, but you should always keep in mind that mining alone is not a profitable alternative so being part of a pool is a better answer.

Is Bitcoin mining difficult?

Currently a finite limit is managed as part of the Bitcoin, these are created by miners, either through individuals or some companies that own mining hardware, so miners receive rewards for their work through the cryptocurrency itself.

But to get to perceive some level of profit you must implement power, since in this way you earn more money by mining at a higher capacity, mining of this type requires specialized machines such as ASICs, since they are the ones that will carry out the computational calculations.

The function of Bitcoin mining follows the same way a decentralized system, therefore mining seeks that each operation is verified, that way you can avoid that there is some kind of payment related to a fraud, but all this requires power for bitcoin mining to be useful and is measured under hash per second or hashrate.

The complication of mining Bitcoin is based on the fact that more computers are integrated to the mining network and this increases the computational capacity of the network, this type of path increases the competition and makes it difficult to find the reward, the difficulty of making any calculation is that the possibility of obtaining blocks occurs every 10 minutes.

In case new blocks are created in less than ten minutes, as was the average in 2016, it is automatically reset, that reset increases the complexity that exists on the puzzles, that is why choosing another type of cryptocurrencies can be a solution in the face of this issue.

www.ingramcontent.com/pod-product-compliance
Lightning Source LLC
Chambersburg PA
CBHW070436220526
45466CB00004B/1707